# THE BIG INSTAGRAM

# SECRET

The Ultimate Guide Playbook to
Grow One Million Followers
Fast, Drive Massive Traffic, and
Become More Profitable

Frank Wilson

1

THE BIG
INSTAGRAM
SECRET
The Ultimate Playbook to Grow One
Million Followers Fast, Drive Massive
Traffic, and Become More Profitable

Frank Wilson

# Copyright

# Table of Contents

# Introduction

Social networking sites, over the years, have experienced incredible growth. With its easy interface, these sites have become sure-shot win to their founders. This does not only refer to websites but also the incredible number of modern mobile applications. These facilitate social networking and are continuously improved for easier accessibility. Instagram is one such networking site with a huge number of users worldwide. You're probably on Instagram or might know somebody else with an Instagram account. Since it was launched, more and more people use the service every day. Everyone from the girl next door to celebrities used their services to increase the visibility of their social media.

You're going to learn all about Instagram in this book. Everything, starting from the fundamental elements of the creation of a service profile to the use of it. Once all the information we have gathered for you is well understood, you can use this platform effectively as easily as you do a pen for business.

# Chapter One: Instagram Niche

It takes series of practical works for you to build up yourself in any kind of business. Whichever product that you are selling or planning to market online or offline, certain factors should be put into consideration to make your competition strong. You need to know the things that set your business apart from other ones and keep working with it. That is why it is essential in any kind of business to have a niche.

A business niche is that area in a broader market that your business is focused on or specialized in to differentiate it from the likes. For any business to survive, it is vital to differentiate your business from others even if the industry or market is saturated.

Discover that underserved or unmet needs in your industry and focus on those areas.

A niche in any business is your specialty, the area that you focus on. It means the expertise that sets you apart from other business persons. Having a clear niche helps you communicate your expertise to your specific target clients. A niche can help you focus on one area. You can get better at it. You can work faster and more efficiently. You can get to know people in that area and ultimately you can make more money. The benefit to you having a niche is that it helps you define the kind of people you want to work with and the kind of work you want to do.

## Niche Selection

Picking up a profitable writing niche is one of the most important things you will do to win clients and improve your business. For you to pick the best niche, you need to start thinking about these three requirements:

1) Your niche should be something that you know about or something that you can learn: I have seen many people hold themselves back like crazy just because they don't feel like they're expert enough to venture into one business or the other. The truth is that there are lots of business niche you don't need years and years of experience, and clients aren't going to grill you about your industry knowledge. All You need is to understand the client's business and make a thorough research to fill in any knowledge gaps.

2) It should be something that you are interested in, something that you know you will enjoy doing a lot: Do not pick a business niche that is going to make you hate your life. You do not want to do that. You don't need those businesses that aren't going to be as profitable as you want. So you have to consider

profitability. Pick a niche that doesn't make you feel like you're waking up being tortured every day. That's not good for you, and it's not suitable for your clients. That's why your business niche should be something that you have a passion for. So that even if you don't get discouraged before the business starts yielding returns.

3) It should be something that a particular kind of target client is willing to pay you well for: This is important because this is the step where you are going to determine the profitability of your writing niche. While trying to discover underserved or unmet needs in industry, also consider if it will yield a profit to cover up for the expenses. Also, ensure that you have accessible target customers for the niche that you're trying to focus on.

Take, for instance, in a large industry of footwear; you can decide to focus on only adult female footwear rather than going into footwear business for adult male and female and children footwear for both male and female. You can be more successful focusing on one niche.

Again, still in the footwear industry, one can decide to focus on canvas of all sizes and for males and females of any age. This is also another way of niche selection in the footwear industry. All you have to do is to think out of the box and know the best much to do your business.

# Chapter Two: Competing Concept: Misunderstood Marketing

Marketing is one of the terms misused in business. Most People think Selling is marketing and marketing is selling, but the truth remains that both are never the same. Marketing is a distinct business philosophy that, when understood and applied properly, will help your business become more profitable.

We have four competing concepts under which publishing companies can successfully carry out their marketing activities. These are very vital concepts in analyzing the customer's needs to be able to satisfy them. They also enable an increase in sales, customer retention, profit maximization, and the ability to deal with competition. These are the production Concept,

13

the Product Concept, the Selling Concept, and the Marketing Concept.

The production Concept explains the fact that consumers will favor those products that are widely available and low in cost. In this case, the focus is on achieving high production efficiency and distribution rather than satisfying the needs of the customers.

The Product Concept can be seen as the "better mousetrap" philosophy, which bases its assumption that good products create their market and so do not need massive marketing expenditure. That is to say that customers are likely to purchase the most quality products in terms of appearance and content. Here the emphasis is usually on the packaging and the quality, thereby losing sight of the fact that the market may be less of an attraction.

The Selling Concept believes that consumers will not buy most of the business products when they are left alone. The company will, therefore, have to embark on an aggressive selling and promotion effort to stimulate buyers into making a purchase. Businesses adhering to this philosophy tend to attract customers through a heavy promotion that brings to focus the features of the products

It can be deduced from These first three viewpoints the needs of the company and its desire to convert a product into cash. And so, the emphasis is on making sales by selling what they have rather than giving what the market wants. This is a short-term outlook that will eventually lead to lower profits and outright failure.

Conversely, the Marketing Concept, which is the fourth concept, is a long-term business philosophy that bases its argument that the key to achieving success is embedded in giving prospective buyers what they want to buy. This will ensure customer retention, as well as customer attraction. While the selling concept starts with the seller and its need for profits, it focuses on its products and considers heavy selling and promoting to sell more products. The marketing concept focuses on an outside-in perspective by starting with a well-defined market, concentrate on customer needs, put into practice all the activities that will affect customers, and makes profits by satisfying customers.

# Chapter Three: Factors for Implementing the Marketing Concept

To be able to understand the marketing concept from scratch and to apply it correctly, you must understand the following factors. These factors are the pillars of the marketing concept and are need for implementing the marketing concept. They included: target market, customer needs, integrated marketing, and profitability.

Identify and define your target market.

Your target market: Who are your target market? Before you begin a venture into any business, know exactly who are the consumers of your products. Your target market is one of the most important factors that you must consider in business. Different market accounts for different products. Therefore, define your target audience. Appealing to your audience should be your number one priority. Therefore, it is essential to know what appeals to your buyers. When you understand what motivates them, that is when you know how to engage them. You also need to have an understanding of the reasons your buyers buy your products and then appeal to those reasons to hook them. The ability to connect with your audience by appealing to them is very vital.

Determine your customers' needs.

This analysis pinpoint segments with widely varying needs. So, the obvious next step to attain is to determine what those needs are. Let's use College Market as a typical example of having various buyers with diverse needs.

In the college market, you will find:

College teachers who are looking for books that could be used as textbooks or for supplementary materials. They seek information that is presented sequentially, discussion questions at the end of each chapter and perhaps with an instruction guide as aid

you will also find

Students who require concise, clear, and inexpensive but relevant books that will give them the facts they need, to get employed without stress.

again,

Career placement officers who need to increase the number of college students that graduate with jobs. are included

also

Alumni associations who need to provide alumni with relevant information that will make their alma mater stand out and increase the donations to the school and

College bookstores that have in mind to make a profit selling books.

All these segments are part of the college market.

Buyers in any one of these segments will have varying needs. Selling to all of them using the same appeal and literature reduces the chance of making or increasing sales. Marketing to them, base on their different needs, will surely yield better results. Having an understanding of the buyers in each of your target segments and marketing to them as an individual will surely result in sales of more goods or services.

Integrated marketing.

Any business adhering to the marketing concept should not end his or her strategizing here. A

Marketer knows that all parts of the marketing process must be coordinated unless he/she wants the result dilute. There are four components of marketing campaigns: the product, its distribution, price, and promotion.

Product. Your product may be a softcover book which you sell on Instagram or Facebook. But the product itself is what your buyer benefits from it. This is what you are selling. It is left for you to decide whether you are selling help, convenience, information, or entertainment. That is what your audience wants and is willing to pay for.

Distribution: this involves how best you can get your products or services to your customers. Some of the steps involved in product or services distribution are transportation, packaging, storage, and advertising. Therefore, you need to decide on how best to make this happen without spending more than you should and, at the same time, satisfying your customers.

Pricing. Pricing under the selling concept is always about matching competitors' prices. Marketing, on the other hand, considers what the customer is willing to pay for the value received. Marketers also make use of non-price incentives like free shipping, bundling, or two-for-one deals to maximize sales.

Promotion. This may be considered the only variable under the selling concept. But, the content and thrust of your promotion (including publicity, direct mail, advertising, sales promotion, and media appearances) depend on your target segment, product differences, distribution strategy, and pricing. A good marketer should be able to answer how these will interact and support one another for maximum effectiveness.

Profitability.

The selling concept stresses profitability to be the goal in business. Any marketer operating under these conditions will seek short-term revenue even if it comes at the expense of long-term success.

A good marketer should be able to understand that even though profitability is essential, it should not be the objective of his or her efforts. Instead, the goal should be on "doing the right things" rather than "doing things right." The intuitive marketer will work at performing all the tasks well that will generate profits, and then profits will come.

Obviously, it is quite clear that there is a significant difference between selling and marketing. A heavy selling campaign, though, will sell some products, but not to be compared to the impact that the targeted marketing campaign will create. Knowing whom you are selling to, what is important to them, how you can integrate all the marketing elements, and then place

23

emphasis on doing the right things. You will sell more products or services and become more profitable in the process.

# Chapter Four: Market Segmentation

Marketing is vital for every business, whether small or a huge commercial body, and so, it has become a significant challenge to market the business products. Every businessperson applies different kinds of marketing strategies that he feels suitable for their business. As the competition is increasing with every passing day, the traditional kind of marketing techniques is no longer enough. No business can operate successfully in every market, nor can the firm always do a good job within one broad market. Businesses do best when they define their target markets and go with a smart structured market plan. For a business to survive, one needs to use marketing segmentation.

Market segmentation is, therefore, a process of choosing a small group of people to market the products or the services of the business. It gives an idea about the demand of the products and services and also helps in lessening the cost of business. The three main reasons why a business person should use the market segmentation for his business are as follows:

It increases the revenue of the business.

Being a business person, you know that not every one of your customers has the same interest in your products; thus, they want to purchase different things. Market segmentation differentiates all customers based on their interests, preference, behavior, location, and so on, depending on the type of business. This helps to lessen the marketing cost and to enhance the sale of business and revenue.

It reduces the cost of business

When a businessperson launches new products and decides to market it to his/her customers, he/she can select a segment that is best for those products. He/she does not need to market to all customers but to specific ones, thus reducing the cost of marketing.

Better customer relationship

With marketing segmentation a businessperson can understand the requirements of the customers separately and can offer the best services or products as according to their needs. This also helps in building better and long-lasting customer relationship.

Market segmentation has to do with dividing a larger market into smaller groups according to characteristics. Because there is a great variety of consumers with different variables, meeting up with their different expectations won't be that effective and might lead to a waste of resources. That's why you need to focus on a few specific consumers that you have a high likelihood or probability of reaching.

Market segmentation is done by businesses to get a more ideal set of characteristics for who their consumers are. Knowing fully well that businesses simply can't target everyone in their marketing efforts because basically their products don't mean the same things to all people. Targeting everyone makes your message dilute because your messages might mean different things to different people. Just like what someone in their early 20s might find interesting, someone in the 50s or 60s is going to find little or no relevance in terms of the impact on their daily lives. That is the reason for engaging in the process called market segmentation that enables businesses to satisfy the needs of their customers better. By targeting everyone, it's challenging to determine the needs of everyone because, many times, they're in direct conflict with one another, but through market segmentation, you can identify a specific group, a specific customer that all have shared characteristics; and then you can develop a message that is much more powerful in reaching that particular group. The purpose of market segmentation is to develop what we call a target market which is a group of people who are most likely to purchase your particular product. Your target market in business is the consumer that you are channeling all of your marketing efforts to attract them and make them purchase your products. That doesn't mean that you wouldn't sell your products to anyone who wanted to purchase them. It means that every of the arrangement that you do, starting from the messages you display, through television, print ads, from the products, are geared towards one type of consumer.

The reason for doing this in businesses is to focus your energies. All products are designed for a particular type of consumer with different income levels, different interests, different backgrounds, different education levels, and all sorts of different variables in the process of market segmentation.

# Chapter Five: Methods Of Market Segmentation

There are four distinct methods to segment a market, that's to take it from a larger group to smaller pieces.

## Demographic segmentation

Demographic segmentation answers the question of Who needs your product or service? It is simply dividing the market into segments based upon certain characteristics that include everything from age to gender, ethnicity, income levels, marital status, education. The goal of demographic segmentation is to cater for a specific group.

For instance: If you have a particular Product that is designed for young adults between 17 to 25 years. These people are most likely to purchase your products and so you have to develop your promotional strategies for them. You wouldn't want to market to everyone because you ultimately know who it's for. Therefore you need to target that specific group and focus on that particular age group. Bearing in mind that 'age' is only but one particular source of segmentation and so there is still a need to split this market up into smaller chunks. You, therefore, take a look at things like income, age, gender, marital status, education. That is to say that there are certain products that people are more inclined to purchase based upon education levels, based upon income levels, and so on. For example, certain classes of cars, certain types of homes are usually reserved for people with certain incomes. So obviously, you wouldn't want to target someone who's not in that particular income level.

In summary, let's assume that you have clothes for teenagers between 13 years to 19 years. Your first demographic segmentation has been done based on age. After segmenting based on age, the next thing is to focus on different segments within that overall group to get more focused. So, you can focus on either male or female teenager of between 13 to 19 year olds that have parents with incomes that are greater than #400,000 because you know that they're going to have more disposable income and that 13 to 19-year-olds are very good at persuading parents. This will enable you to develop a very effective message for reaching this particular group.

## Geographic segmentation.

It answers the question of Where are your customers?

Geographic segmentation is looking at the places that people live and focusing on people that reside in certain areas. By using geographic segmentation, the market is divided into segments based upon where consumers live. So you look at things based upon urban versus rural areas because obviously, people that live in urban areas may have a different need from someone who lives in a rural area. There is also a need to consider locations around the globe, not just simply rural versus urban areas. You can also look at population density, climates, and weather conditions in that area. For example, in certain areas of the country, the kind of dress to sell will differ from the other because of the climatic change.

Geographic segmentation therefore is dividing the market into groups based upon geographical location and so you may do this on a regional basis or based upon zip code and a host of other areas. The main thing with geographic segmentation and usually why most marketers incorporate it to some degree is because it clearly shows the level on which a marker or company operates. A marketer with a limited number of resources can't necessarily target an entire state or nation. So it's essential to focus on their specific local community. Therefore, based on the kind of products you deal on, you will be able to know where exactly to find your ideal customers, which is where your product has more use.

## Psychographic segmentation:

It answers the question of Why do your customers make the choices they make?

Knowing that maybe the product that you sell is geared towards females and you did your segmentation based upon that group. Afterward, you segmented based upon income. And so you're going to keep segmenting until you get a small group that has the highest probability of purchasing your product.

Therefore, in addition to demographic segmentation and geographic Segmentation, psychographic segmentation focuses on a more impactful group and also divides the market into smaller groups based on interests, lifestyles, that are focusing based on "Like". It addresses the problems with Geographic and demographic segmentation by looking at characteristics that may predict purchasing decisions. There's a great deal of variability of lifestyles and interests you can have. For example, Fitness/Body-centered, Materialist, Hedonist, Service/Spiritual, Technocrat, and Academic/Intellectual are all types of lifestyle, but even within that, you can have individuals of any of these lifestyles, but with certain incomes; of academic level, but with psychographic segmentation, you Focus on secondary school students which is a more specific group than simply teenagers of between 13- 19 years which is general secondary school students age range. Facebook, which we all probably know, does a great job of focusing on lifestyles, attitudes, and interests because a Facebook account gathers much information about us for selling and advertising. Psychographic segmentation, in essence, is much more effective than simply demographic and geographic segmentation because you're not just looking at the actual makeup and characteristics of people instead, you're looking more at what they are interested in to predict purchasing decisions.

## Behavioral segmentation:

It ask the question of How do your customers behave?

Obviously, there is a flaw with regards to psychographic segmentation which is, that it is by assumption and assuming that if you have a certain lifestyle if you are between 17-19 year if you're located in a specific region, that you are more inclined to make purchasing decisions which are most likely to be so. However it's not a guaranteed thing and so marketers ultimately want to make sure that the money that is spent on those things is done in an effective manner. This is why marketers do engage in behavioral segmentation which goes beyond lifestyles, interest, attitudes of a particular audience/market, but to look specifically at consumers' behavior towards various products to divide the market into more smaller segment. Take, for instance, Amazon, which is an online market place that offers different services, and products became so successful because they engage in behavioral segmentation. When you purchase something via Amazon from time to time, at some point in time, you'll notice that they offer you similar products based upon your purchasing behavior which is much more effective because you're targeting people ultimately based upon what they do or engage in rather than what they say they will do. So if you target people based upon their ultimate behavior, it's much more effective because behavior is indicative of what one truly want, what one is particularly interested in. If I purchase books for example related to a certain discipline let's say I purchased books that are related to the field of economics and Amazon sees this, what they will do is to advertised similar books that have a background in economics in some way, shape or form because they feel that if I purchase something before related to that field I'm probably interested in that and so I'm probably going to purchase similar things again.

In summary, you can use each of these four methods to segment your target market from the total market to have an ideal set of characteristics of the consumer that you are targeting, whom your product is designed for. With market segmentation, you will know what they like, what they're interested in, what they are looking for in a product to ideally design something specifically for them. That's the main goal. Creating something and then finding someone to sell it to is very effective. So it works best to know who is your market first, who are you trying to target, finding out what they like. What drives them? What's the pain in the market that they feel from not having a particular need met? And then designing something as a way of fulfilling that particular need. By engaging in market segmentation, not only do you get a good idea of who your consumer is but you also know-how; and how to design products and services ultimately with their needs in mind(by writing books that solve, human problem). From this, you can be able to say that I am selling for female adults who earn not less than #100,000 monthly in the eastern part of the world.

They must be graduates and, most importantly, those that like wearing fashionable footwear or clothes.

# Chapter Six: Targeting/ Target Marketing

Once you've defined a potential audience for your ebook coupled with segmentation, your next step is to determine how to reach that audience. Do any magazines or journals target that specific group? Does the group have a professional organization, or some other source of "membership," that could provide you with a list of members? Are there special stores that members of this group might visit? Can you find discussion groups and major websites for this group? The answers to these questions will enable you determine how easy (or how difficult) it will be to get your message to the right customers. Based on this, there are two most important ways of targeting online.

## Behavioral targeting

Technology has increased the use of behavioral targeting. Behavioral targeting in an online environment is a database-driven marketing system that monitors consumers' behavior to find out his or her interests so as to be able to serve ads to that person with relevance to those interests. For example, if an individual spent time on fashion websites looking up prices of clothes, it could be inferred that that person needs to buy clothes. He or she could receive ads from designers company or whatever webpages he or she visits. Behavioral targeting requires marketers to make use of their media strategies thereby, shifting from traditional media which involves the use of television, magazines, radio, newspapers, and outdoor to reach a mass audience to media such as the Internet, direct mail, text and video messages, that can directly reach consumers and even more efficiently.

## Geo-targeting

A marketer can now target customers based on where they live. When online, you can determine an individual's physical location and send messages to a website visitor based on his or her location. In this targeting, it involves customizing an advertisement for a product or service to a particular market depending on the geographic location of potential buyers. This location can include any of these: country, province, city, or postal code, therefore, allowing a marketer to specify whether or not ads will be shown on a website based on the searcher's location. Such technology allows local marketers and smaller marketers with limited financial means to compete more effectively with larger marketers who have far greater resources. Mobile technology is also shaping individual targeting practices. Your smartphone has the ability to track down individuals while they are on the move. By sending messages across, you can find buyers of your eBook.

# Chapter Seven: Setting up Your Instagram Business Account

Instagram is one of the biggest and one of the best social media networks on the market, with over one billion active monthly users and 25 million active business accounts. Since the creation of Instagram in 2010, it has grown with over 80 million photos being shared on wants daily basis as well as over 500 million activities being varied out on it. As such, it has become one of the most popular website to promote businesses. It's obvious they're not going anywhere anytime soon. In this chapter, you will learn how you can create an Instagram business account, grow your following fast, tell stories to win your audience's attention and maximize sales, use hash tags effectively, and so on.

Setting up your Instagram business account is a simple thing to do, though requires you to be creative. Business account gives you access to extra features that are lacking on a personal account. These additional features allow easy promoting of your business products and services.

If you already have a personal Instagram account which you would want to switch to a business account, this is what you will do:

- Log into your account
- tap the little man symbol located at the bottom right of the screen to open up your profile
- tap on the will setting icon located on the top right-hand side

- List of options will open, scroll down to see the option " switch to a business profile," and tap it.

- The next screen will open, directing you through the process of setting up your business account.

- Click on continue. A series of screens that tell you more about the advantages of switching to a business account will keep appearing. Keep going till you get to the last screen.

- On that screen, you will be asked to connect to your Facebook business account. That's if you have one. If you do, choose the option, but if you don't, ignore it. Click on next

- Confirm your details including your email address, phone number, business address.

- Click done, a popup message asking you to go to your profile will appear. Click on the go to profile button.

- Add your profile picture that depicts your business

- Add your name, username, website link or WhatsApp link on the website option

- Add a short but compelling Bio. I will come to this later in another chapter

- Add email address, phone number, and select gender if you want

- Check the "similar account suggestions box

- Click submit.

For newbies on Instagram, all you have to do is to register with your email and password. Once you're done, log in and edit your profile, as illustrated above.

# Chapter eight: Growing Instagram Following

Instagram is an amazing tool for business because engagement is higher on it than on any other social media platform. You only need a thousand followers to start seeing an impact on your account. This is based on the concept of a thousand true fans, if you have a thousand people who truly care about what you're saying you can have a successful business.

Below is how you can gain a thousand Instagram followers to your account.

Step 1- Define and know who your target followers are. Bearing in mind of the previous topics we've discussed so far, you don't need everyone on the platform. You need to get super clear on who would be the perfect follower for you to have. Are they male or female? What interests do they have? How do they spend their free time? When are they on their phone using Instagram? What kind of posts do they like and engage with? You need to take time to write these down, and then you provide the answers to these questions.

Step 2- Get your bio on point

There are multiple parts of the bio, including your name field, bio section, call to action section, and URL.

Your name field is searchable on Instagram. Therefore, in the name field, you want to have the top keywords that you want your target market to use to find you, even if that's just your brand's name.

The next section is the bio section. The first line of your bio section should talk directly to your target audience about the value they will get for following you. It involves what they can expect by following you. Tell them in that first line and elaborate on that in the second line. Take time, though in the shortest period to share a little bit more about why you're different.

Then the last part of the bio is the call to action section. In this section of the bio, you don't want your Instagram followers to be passive, you want them to websites be clicking the link in your bio. To ensure that, make the very last line of your bio a clear specific call to action as to why they should click on your link. What's in it for them; a new blog post; a free resource; will they see one of your videos? Literally, tell them in your call to action why they should click on your link.

The last part of your Instagram bio is a URL. You need to have a link to where you're going to send your Instagram traffic. Instagram is the top of your funnel so what next step do you want someone to take in your business? Is it to go to your blog, your service page, or just your home page.

Step 3- Hashtag

Using the hashtags that your target follower is also using. Since you already know who your target market is, you need to get into their head. What are the hashtags that they're using? What do they care about? What are the community bonding hashtags that they're adding on to their posts? It would help if you took some time to do this research. You can do this by heading to Your Instagram using your desktop. Type in tohashtag and your keywords into the search bar. You're going to see a bunch of suggestions popping right underneath your keyword. Scroll through those hashtags and choose the ones that are relevant to your target audience. In carrying out your hashtag research keep on going until you find not less than 30 hashtags that your target follower cares about.

Step four- build a content bank

Creating a content bank will save you many headaches if you have a folder of images or copies that you can access when you need to post. These images could come from your photography, stock imagery, or you can also source out images. Keep all of your images organized in a Dropbox or Google Drive folder. The cool thing about these softwares is that they both have corresponding apps so that you can access these images very easily on your phone.

Step five- Forming a team.

The next step to gaining your next 1,000 Instagram followers is by teaming up with others in your niche. Yes, they could be your competitors, but you all can be a support for each other and stay accountable to each other. Team up with others in your niche and stick to it together. Agree to hold each other accountable. You can keep this really simple and just have an Instagram DM thread you can create a WhatsApp or telegram group or you can create a Facebook Messenger thread. The key is to agree to post there and keep each other accountable.

# Chapter Nine: Marketing Strategies on Instagram

For your business, you can better use the platform to connect and convert your ideal customer and client. In this chapter, we are going to be learning about the latest and greatest marketing strategies, tools, tips, tricks, and tactics.

Optimizing your bio.

Just like we discussed in the previous chapter, the very first thing you do on Instagram, whether you're just getting started or whether you're looking to take your account to the next level is, , could be done by describing accurately,

clearly; you and concisely what you do and who you do it for. Also, talk about why your account is worth someone's attention and time? Of course, if you've got them there, you've compelled them with what you do and whom you do it for and why you're worth following. Follow them up with calls to action. Also, add links as well as free materials, as discussed before. You can use a link tracker like Bitly to see how many people are clicking the link you attached to your bio.

Creating a brand plan.

The three words that can help you build an effective brand plan are consistency, clarity and congruence.

Consistency means that you're applying a regular schedule; that's making sure that you're posting regularly, you're checking in regularly, responding to comments, and responding to DMs on a regular and consistent schedule. All of these help to prove that you're a reliable and trustworthy brand. Clarity is all about what you're about, your style, and what you do and making sure that is, exactly what you do, whom you do it for, why you're worth following as already covered. Also, the theme, tone, and style across your entire account also matter. Confusing someone is

one of the quickest ways to lose them no matter what. Lastly is congruence; that's, making sure that what you do, what you talk about, what you post, and all the images work together and follow the same line and theme.

You are leveraging on both feed and stories in your Instagram marketing plan.

Stories and feedback, if you master them, can enhance your conversions from possible customers, build a space for you on Instagram, and improve your visual communication. Since most people are used to scanning through the web, therefore, instead of reading them, stories and feedbacks always stand out and so will engage your audience. Interactive stories and corporate stories can link points and help people read and take action. You can start captivating your target market by creating emotional connections with all your content to maximize your potential customer conversions. How other people see you can be affected by fascinating stories. How they perceived you determines whether or not they will read your blog posts or comment on them, they will refer people to your business.

If you're running Instagram ads, you can leverage

both feeds and stories and see which one provides a better return on investment for you and your business.

Hashtags.

So many people are still missing the

boat in leveraging and using hashtags across all of their posts. It's so important because this is how people are going to be finding you and your content.

The first tip when it comes to hashtags to help to elevate your game and get more bank for your buck is to do hash research, as discussed earlier. The next tip is to vary those pile if hashtags you've got over time. The reason is to enable you to continue showing up in front of new and varied audiences by using a variety of different hashtags. If you stick to the same hashtag over and over again, your account will only be showing up in front of the same people again and again. The effect of this is that your account is going to be stagnate and not grow as much as it would do when you vary the people that you're trying to reach.

Leveraging on a micro-influencer strategy.

I know you've heard of influencer marketing where celebrities and people with large accounts go out there and get paid to promote a product on their feed. But there's a sub-segment of this massive industry known as micro-influencers, and this is where I'd recommend you really want to start diving with. Micro-influencers are niche-specific businesses or people with tiny audiences of the exact perfect people that you're trying to reach. By going after them, you're able to often get incredibly cost-effective placements and postings and reach the who you're trying to reach. But of course, finding the right micro-influencer is going to take a little bit of digging and a little bit of research. Still, well worth the effort.

That user-generated content.

Leveraging user-generated content is a fantastic way to build brand loyalty, build engagement with your tribe and also take a little bit of the load off your plate when it comes to creating content. Fortunately, generating user generated content is a bit of a mouthful since it's easier than you might think All you need to do is ask for it and one of the best

and easiest ways to do this is by using a submissions page right on your website which you can direct people to. People submit content, you review it and you post it and give them a shout out, and that's it.

Using paid promotions.

If you've got a business, and you want to generate more leads, customers and sales, you're going to leverage the incredible power of Instagram ads. This does a couple really cool things for your business. The first of which is that it allows you to keep your organic feed free from all promotions because you're going to be able to supplement that with paid advertising. The second thing is that understanding that Instagram ads are one of the most powerful advertising tools available today because they're owned by Facebook ads which as we all know has one of the most powerful advertising algorithms available, allowing you to pinpoint your exact ideal target market and put your message directly in front of them. If you've got a business that's trying to generate more leads, customers, and sales, you should be using Instagram ads.

# Chapter Ten: Storytelling for your Instagram

People are born to love stories and visual communication. Storytelling gives life meaning and makes an emotional connection, creates ecstasy, sorrow, or peace sensations, and attracts your audience. True stories makes your work to be perceived as authentic just exactly the same way live events get retweets. Your content will far impact your audience or viewers as well as improve your credibility. That's exactly what you need in terms of your marketing strategy for social media. Sharing success stories and stories of mistakes can develop your relationship with potential customers. That is why it is very necessary to use relevant images as well as great visual stories when you write. This is because it peak people's interest. Likewise, if when recording a podcast, it is of a great importance that you use emotion-triggering music and sounds. And, for video creation, using, words, imaged, sounds, and visual stories can do the magic.

Visual communication

Visual story is a means of letting your mind, emotions, and thoughts known to your target audience using visual, that's, images to make emotional connection. Infographics, videos, memes, screenshots are all examples of visual stories and communication that is widely used on major social media websites, including Instagram. You can also create and upload visual stories and contents to major media sites and channels, including Animoto, Vimeo, and Slideshare. This lets you meet a larger target audience for your business and future customers.

# Elements of storytelling

Storytelling is so powerful that fires our imaginations and stirs our emotions. It moves us into taking actions and it enables us to communicate and rapport with our target market most effectively. But to do justice to the act of storytelling, you must ensure the following:

Entertaining.

Your story should be good enough to keep your audience engaged and focus so they can anticipate what's coming next.

Educational.

Educational stories leads to curiosity among your audience. In addition to that, it will be a source of knowledge to them. Ensure that your readers acquired new information or knowledge after listening or seeing your story.

Universal.

Any good stories shouldn't impact only your target market. Instead, it should be something that any reader can benefit from. It should be able to give hope to any reader irrespective of the niche.

Organization.

Organized stories easily get to the emotions of your audience. It brings about smooth understanding and assimilation of the story.

Memorable.

Plan your story very well to ensure it sticks to your audience's mind.

# Process of story telling

Know your audience

Who would want to listen to your story? Who will your story impact or benefit? Before you begin any story, be sure that you know and understand your target market very well. Your target market are the ones to take action; therefore, try to know what they want to be able to create compelling stories that move them.

Define your core message

Every story, no matter how long it is or the number of page it has, there should be a central core of thought, that's the core message the story is trying to pass. You need to establish the message. What's your story about? Is your story explain a service? Is it selling a product? To ensure that your story has a core message, summarize your entire story in a few sentences. If you're unable to do so, it means that your story has no core message.

Decide the kind of story you want to tell

Stories are created differently to elicit the kind of feelings you want from your readers. Having this in mind, you will be able to determine the exact story that will move your audience. This can also be achieved by knowing the objective of your storytelling. For instance, if your story is to....

-incite action, you will have to include how that same action or a similar one was achieved. Then include the process that made that possible and the benefits that resulted from taking that action.

- tell who you are, your story should have to feature your genuineness, your struggles, failures, and wins. This increases your authenticity.

-convey values; your story should include familiar character, emotions, situations to ensure they understand ways of applying the story to their life.

-foster collaboration, your story in this regard should be able to move your readers into discussing your story with other people. Use words like "me too" to explain experience that your readers can relate to.

- impact knowledge or educate such stories should include trial-and-error experience and a win experience to a problem. This will teach your audience how to handle similar problems using your method. Also, include alternative ways of solving problems.

Establish call-to-action

A call to action urges your audience to take the next step after listening to your story. This enables your audience not only listen to your story, instead, take action after listening. Your call to action should tell the audience what you expect of them. It must be simple and actionable. You can use such words like:

Start My Free Trial Now

Get More Details

Share Now

Leave a Review

Tap the share button below

Subscribe Here, and so on

Remember that not including a CTAs is just like not crossing the finish line after running a marathon race. Any of these calls to actions should be used depending on the objective of the storytelling.

# Chapter Eleven: Story Tips for Media Appearance

Media appearances give an amazing opportunity of getting the message you have to a large audience with a limited period. That you're on a show isn't a guarantee that your book will sell. You need to be aware of the content as well as the delivery of your message. Below are guidelines that will enable you to pass your message quickly to your audience with immediate call to actions:

1) Creative. Since your audience is preoccupied with many activities that may distort or inhibit your intended message, you quickly need to break through to them by being exceptional, though in an entertaining way. Making use of an innovative approach gets and engages your audience's attention.

For example, introduce unexpected or new information. Give a new angle on what is already known. Capture the imaginations of the people in the audience with a twist on what they anticipate, and you will have them in the palm of your hand.

2)Credible. A guest is not looked upon as an objective spokesperson, and the audience naturally expects you to say only what is good about your book or product. Introduce yourself to your audience in a way that will position you as an objective source of information. This is to let the audience know you have the qualifications to make statements about this topic, and you should be taken seriously. Being perceived as an ulterior motive makes you suspect in your viewers' minds immediately. Combat that by using real-life illustrations. It can be more impacting if the instances are personal, that's, describing and expressing your personal experience. Give your audience the reasons to empathize with you. Let them know how you survived, conquered, the methods you implemented, your discoveries, proves, what they will gain by following your advice, and how they can.

Don't try to impress your audience with how much you know. You don't have to emphasize over even if you help people in the past if you or even if you know what you are saying. Let them know that you are not there to impress them, instead to help them overcome some problems they are facing or they might face in the future. All you have to do is to know who you are and speak from your heart.

3)Convincing. The truth is that things that are true are not always believable, and believable things are not always true. Document your words by providing enough details to be able to convince your audience that you are saying nothing but the truth. You can achieve this by presenting charts and figures to document your speech story.

4) Clarity. Do not beat around the bush. In many cases, people listen to your audios while busy things. Grab their attention with an immediate, positive impact to heed what you are saying. You should be concise, clear, and accessible. Translate your message in a way your audience can understand what you are saying. Make simple, direct answers that are understandable to the lowest common denominator. Be natural, friendly and informative.

# Conclusion

I believe that you've learnt a lot on how to skyrocket your business on Instagram. All you need to do is to put into practice all that you've learnt. One thing am assuring you is that if you do them correctly, you will experience a massive turn around in your business.

Thanks.

Remember to leave a review.